SCARECROWS

"No eye hath seen such Scarecrows"

WILLIAM SHAKESPEARE

SCARECROWS

COLIN GARRATT

MILEPOST

The pictures in this book have been made by Colin Garratt on the brilliant range of high resolution films from Agfa, including the new HDC Colour Print and CTX colour transparency films which have been widely acclaimed for their tolerant stable emulsions and vibrant colours. Canon Eos cameras and lenses have also been used for their brilliance of definition and the pictures made with lenses ranging from 24mm to 600mm.

This edition first published 1995 by Milepost Publishing
in conjunction with Arcturus Limited and exclusively for
Bookmart Limited
Desford Road, Enderby, Leicester, LE9 5AD

Milepost Publishing is a division of Milepost 92½,
Milepost 92½ is Colin Garratt's Audio Visual, Production,
Presentation and Photographic Service for the Railway Industry
incorporating The Railway Picture Library
Originated, Printed and Bound in the UK by Gresham Print Group, Nottingham.
Designed by Milepost / wilson design associates

ISBN 1 900193 10 8

Milepost 92½
Newton Harcourt
Leicestershire
LE8 9FH
Tel 0116 2592068

MILEPOST

INTRODUCTION

The Scarecrow is a relic of medieval times which continues to haunt the landscape. It seems to appear from nowhere and disappears equally mysteriously.

It's origin is obscure, but there is a belief that Scarecrows are derived from the pagan practice of slaughtering humans as a sacrifice to nature; Scarecrows being created as a more civilised successor to the practice.

The Scarecrow's capacity to frighten predators soon became obvious, although once again, there was a parallel human activity as young boys or old men long past retirement, were employed either to work in association with, or instead of, the traditional Scarecrow. These human versions spent their days roaming the crop fields with rattles and clappers to ensure that marauding flocks of birds were kept at bay.

The combination of a human-like presence, combined with movement and sound, became an established ideal and remains in evidence today in Scarecrows with loose clothing and streamers along with cans and bottles which blow and rattle in the wind.

Scarecrows are known by other names; Mawkin, Jack of Straw, Tattybogle Shoyhoy, Jack-a-Lent and Hodmadod.

The name Scarecrow is something of a parody, as they are more effective in warding off pigeons. These are potentially far more troublesome than crows and if left to run amok can ravage a crop, especially during winter when they move around in huge flocks.

Over recent years, a plethora of modern and sophisticated bird scaring devices have been made which should have rendered the traditional Scarecrow extinct, especially as their effectiveness is difficult to measure. They are certainly capable of frightening humans and have often acquired a sinister role in literature and films. There are occasions when Scarecrows hung from trees to sway in the wind have been sighted from a distance, assumed to be a suicide and the police called to the scene. There was a recent newspaper report of a farmer being ordered by the local authority to remove two Scarecrows; apparently the grotesque, gun toting apparitions had alarmed local children and ramblers.

One night, I was filming several scarecrows in a particularly lonely place. The moon was shining, bathing the landscape in a half light. Absorbed in my task, I inadvertently backed up to a particularly hideous looking example and

half turned to find it leering over my shoulder. In the instant my blood ran cold, so instinctive was the feeling that the Scarecrow had moved towards me.

Whether life-like or abstract, the Scarecrow is an intrinsic part of the rural scene; a silent sentinel enacting a spell of duty and transforming the landscape with its presence. Scarecrows have changed little over the centuries, although they are certainly better dressed today, as years ago, vagrants and tramps were quick to strip them of any clothes worth wearing. One significant aspect of evolution is the use of plastic containers, along with other modern materials such as masks and boiler suits.

Scarecrows do exist as families with distinct generic similarities although, like humans, no two are ever alike. These families are to be found in localised areas. There are also very distinct regional variations and, of course, national ones too.

I have attempted to capture the Scarecrow on film as a part of nature. Nowhere will any reference to humans be seen; the fifty Scarecrows in this book populating their own space; some of the pictures could, in theory, have been taken centuries ago – there being nothing present to suggest any point in history.

Neither can any of the pictures be located topographically; each Scarecrow lives out its ephemeral secret, as transient as a passing cloud. And herein lies the key to the photography; for it is the passing cloud, a puff of wind, a ray of sunlight or a raging storm which animates and glorifies them.

The following extract from my diary outlines one particular Scarecrow adventure; the date was April 11th 1989. "It was a blustery, sunny evening with the sky bedecked in heavy cumulus clouds. The Scarecrow stood silhouetted on the brow of a hill presiding in terrifying starkness over the rolling acres; the sun would set behind him. The wind blew like a tornado; it was bitterly cold. I feared the apparition would blow over, but he stood firm flapping slightly. The sunset welled up in high drama with huge bands of dark clouds interlacing the sky through which shafts of golden sunlight appeared. The picture needed to be made from a low angle and I lay in wet sticky mud for over an hour until the drama gave way to twilight. Then, with fingers blue from the cold, I turned into the biting wind and made my way back from that wild place."

Colin Garratt,
Milepost 92 ½,
Newton Harcourt,
Leicestershire,
England.

The lengthening days and ripening crops eloquently
signify that the Scarecrow's work is done. Few remain
to see their task fulfilled for if blown over or obscured
by the crop they are likely to become entangled in the
harvesting machinery and cause serious damage.
Those that do remain through summer are usually
protecting peas, beans or cabbages.

At the beginning of the year, Scarecrows preside over early sowings of rape and wheat. It is a time when the weather is most inclement; battering winter gales, driving rain and sleet, or damp, cold mists. Many Scarecrows get blown into weird positions like drunken men; others collapse and vanish from view. Some stand firm only to be partially dismembered by the wind with pieces of their anatomy spread far and wide. It is not un-common for passers-by to attack a Scarecrow; stabbing and mutilations being the most common.

It is always a great thrill to approach a new Scarecrow.
Will it have a face? Will it be sinister, happy, sad, aggressive,
fiendish, stupid or just a friendly fool? Some of those who
create Scarecrows believe that a face with an expression is
an important factor in deterring predators; others are content
with more abstract forms. It is well known that some of the
most carefully made Scarecrows complete with a face are
stolen, literally vanishing in the night.

It is generally assumed that Scarecrows are male;
their tough lonely vigils and aggressive postures being
unsuited to the fairer sex. Traditionally this was so,
but more females are witnessed today. Rippling dresses
and long billowing hair are relevant to the task and
examples are seen which exude an unmistakable sexual
presence every bit as potent as the fearsome aggression
of their male counterparts. Shop window mannequins
provocatively attired have been recorded acting as
scarecrows and even triggered off a fashion trend during
the 1980s known as the "Scarecrow Look".

When amongst Scarecrows, one gets an uneasy
feeling of being watched. Some are so realistic and
menacing that they appear to be alive. Film makers
and writers have always recognised this. Criminals
have hidden in them. Murderers and spies have
imitated the Scarecrow in motionless disguise as their
would-be captors pass by at close quarters. Dead
bodies have been hidden inside Scarecrows and
stolen loot stashed in the pockets of their great coats.

Scarecrows with guns make convincing marksmen.
With generations of birds having been shot at since
time immemorial, it may be assumed that a figure
with a gun is the ideal deterrent. If his body swivels
round in the wind enabling the gun to be pointed in
all directions so much the better. Most gun bearing
Scarecrows are made with great conviction and
represent a preferable alternative to the degrading
practice of shooting birds.

The Scarecrow has long been associated with mysticism and ritual. In America, they are said to come alive on Halloween Night. Some are reputed to host evil spirits with "eyes that follow children down country lanes at dusk". Walter de la Mare tells of a Scarecrow which frightened both crows and men; "the way it bore itself up was more than you would expect from sticks and rags". The vile apparition turned out to be the ghost of a man who took possession of the Scarecrow to gain his revenge on a rival.

The variety of Scarecrows is infinite and all have
their character. Some stand with arms and legs stiff,
others are a ripple of movement, some root into the
ground like a tree, others stride across the fields
waving flags. Yet more hang from gibbets, twisted
into hideous shapes; others are hoisted on poles.
From Medieval times, the classic location was on
the brow of a hill eerily silhouetted against the sky;
a warning presence by day and a frightening spectre
at dusk. Without the Scarecrow's haunting
presence, our landscape would be greatly
impoverished.